Fact Finders®

ENERGY REVOLUTION

HYDROPOWER

By Mary Boone

Consultant: Ellen Anderson
Executive Director of the Energy Transition Lab
Institute on the Environment
University of Minnesota, Twin Cities

CAPSTONE PRESS
a capstone imprint

Fact Finders Books are published by Capstone Press,
1710 Roe Crest Drive, North Mankato, Minnesota 56003
www.capstonepub.com

Library of Congress Cataloging-in-Publication Data
Names: Boone, Mary, 1963– author.
Title: Hydropower / by Mary Boone.
Description: North Mankato, Minnesota: Fact Finders, an imprint of Capstone
    Press, [2019] | Series: Fact finders. Energy revolution | Includes
    bibliographical references and index. | Audience: Age 9. | Audience: Grades 4 to 6.
Identifiers: LCCN 2018040990 (print) | LCCN 2018042525 (ebook) |
    ISBN 9781543555493 (eBook PDF) | ISBN 9781543555431 (library binding) |
    ISBN 9781543559095 (pbk.)
Subjects: LCSH: Hydroelectric power plants—Juvenile literature. |
    Water-power—Juvenile literature.
Classification: LCC TK1081 (ebook) | LCC TK1081 .B66 2019 (print) | DDC 333.91/4—dc23
LC record available at https://lccn.loc.gov/2018040990

Editorial Credits
Mandy Robbins, editor; Terri Poburka, designer; Jo Miller, media researcher;
Kathy McColley, production specialist

Image Credits
Alamy: imageBROKER, 23, Robert Matton AB, 27, Xinhua, 24-25; Getty Images: Langevin Jacques/Contributor, 17, (inset); iStockphoto: MarioGuti, 20; Newscom: Xinhua Agency/Pan Siwei, 29; Shutterstock: 3xy, 9, A. Aleksandravicius, 15 (top), Aleks Kend, 19, Ariel Ukulele, 26, bubblea, 15; (bottom), Canadapanda, 21, Edmund Lowe Photography, 10-11, Evgeny Vorobyev, 8, Hampi, 25, lexaarts, 16-17, Looka, 7, maxi_kore, 13, Nick_Nick, 6, Rigucci, 22, snapgalleria, 11, stocksolutions, Cover, Tom Wang, 4-5

Design Elements
Shutterstock: HAKKI ARSLAN, T.Sumaetho

Printed and bound in the USA
PA48

TABLE OF CONTENTS

WHAT IS HYDROPOWER?

You drink water. You water your garden. You go for a swim in it. But did you know people can also use water to make electricity?

Hydro is the Greek word for "water." Hydropower uses water to make electricity. Hydropower is also called hydroelectricity. It is a **renewable** energy source.

Renewable energy is made using resources that cannot be used up. Solar power comes from the sun. Wind power comes from the wind. Geothermal power comes from heat inside the earth. These are all forms of renewable energy.

Coal, oil, and natural gas are nonrenewable resources. These fossil fuels take hundreds of millions of years to form. At some point, these fuel sources will be used up.

renewable—describes power from sources that you can use over and over again that cannot be used up, such as wind, water, and the sun

HYDROPOWER THROUGHOUT HISTORY

Hydropower is not new. People have used waterpower for more than 2,000 years. Ancient Greeks used flowing water to turn paddle wheels. The wheels helped grind wheat into flour. By the 1700s water was powering grain, lumber, iron, and fabric mills. The earliest paddle wheels were wooden. During the 1700s people began using larger iron wheels. These bigger paddle wheels could make more power. That meant factories could make more goods in less time.

An old mill still stands along the river in Bayeux, France.

The first mills used the power of the water to do work. But they could not store that energy as electricity.

Soon scientists learned how to use hydropower to create electricity. The world's first hydroelectric project powered a single lamp in England in 1878. Four years later, the world's first hydroelectric power plant began operating. It was located in Appleton, Wisconsin. The plant provided its own power needs and supplied power to two nearby buildings. By 1886 there were between 40 and 50 hydropower plants in North America.

HYDROPOWER TODAY

Today hydropower is the world's most popular type of renewable energy. Hydropower plants range in size. The largest plants can make enough power for more than 20,000 households. Micro plants may create just enough power for one home or farm. There are more than 8,200 large hydropower plants around the world.

The Krasnoyarsk Dam in Russia supplies power to the nearby aluminum plant.

POWERED BY THE WATER CYCLE

Hydropower relies on the earth's natural water cycle. The water cycle includes:

Evaporation – Energy from the sun warms water on the earth. Some of the water turns into **vapor**. This is called evaporation. Plants and trees also lose water through their leaves. This process is called transpiration.

Condensation – As water vapor rises, it cools and turns back into liquid. The liquid joins with particles in the air to form clouds.

Precipitation – When the drops in the clouds become too heavy for the air to hold them, they fall back to the earth as rain, snow, hail, or sleet.

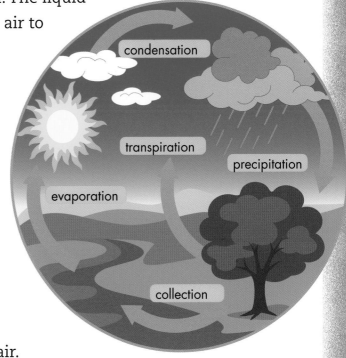

Collection – When precipitation falls, it flows into oceans, rivers, lakes, and ponds.

Eventually, this water evaporates back into the air. Then the cycle starts again.

....

vapor—a gas made from a liquid

CHAPTER 2

HOW CAN WATER MAKE ELECTRICITY?

FACT

Washington makes more hydroelectricity than any other U.S. state. The state's Grand Coulee Dam is the largest source of hydroelectricity in the nation. One-fourth of Washington's electricity comes from hydropower each year.

You have probably been taught that water and electricity don't mix. For example, blow drying your hair in the bathtub is an awful idea. If you drop the dryer in the water, it could cause a shock or even death. So how can water be used to make electricity?

Hydropower isn't dangerous because water does not actually touch the electricity. At most hydropower plants, water is held behind a dam. This water forms an artificial lake called a reservoir. Hydropower plants contain **turbines** that look like fans or propellers. When water is released from the reservoir, it falls through a large pipe. The water spins the turbine blades. The turbines connect to **generators** that also spin. The generators make electricity as they spin. **Transformers** help balance how much electricity is sent out of the plant. Power lines carry the electricity to nearby cities and rural areas.

turbine—a machine with blades that can be turned by a moving fluid such as steam or water

generator—a machine used to convert mechanical energy into electricity

transformer—a device that changes the force of an electrical current

How much electricity a hydropower plant makes depends on how much water flows through the dam and how far it falls. A large, fast river carries more energy than a small, slow one. Also, water falling from a high point, such as Niagara Falls in New York, can produce more energy than a smaller waterfall. For this reason, most hydropower plants are located in hills or mountains.

Freezing winter temperatures can affect hydropower plants. Large plants usually have very deep reservoirs. Even if there is ice on the top, the water toward the bottom keeps flowing. Power plants on smaller waterways do not work well in cold weather. The water at these plants often freezes solid in the winter. Smaller plants located in cold climates usually work only during warm weather.

The water in Niagara Falls drops nearly 200 feet (61 meters) in some places.

There are three types of hydropower plants. Figuring out which type is right for an area depends on land features, climate, and energy needs.

Impoundment – This type of plant is also called a "reservoir" system. It is the most common type of hydropower plant. These plants use dams to store river water in reservoirs. When water is released, it flows through turbines. They spin a generator to make electricity. Dam gates adjust to allow more or less water to flow through.

Diversion – These are also known as "run of the river" plants. They have no reservoirs. They generate power using the natural flow of river water to spin turbines.

Pumped Storage – Pumped storage plants work like giant batteries. They can combine solar, wind, and hydropower. When the sun is shining and the wind is blowing, extra electricity can be produced from wind and solar power. Pumped storage plants make use of this extra power. Pumps powered by the extra wind and solar electricity bring water from a lower reservoir to a higher reservoir. When more power is needed, water is released back into the lower reservoir through turbines.

FACT

Pumped storage plants can also be used with nuclear power.

The Kruonis Pumped Storage Hydroelectric Plant is located in Lithuania.

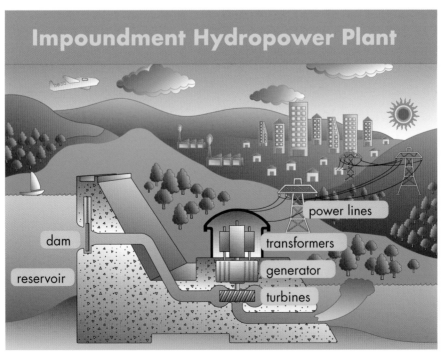

Impoundment Hydropower Plant

power lines

transformers

dam

generator

reservoir

turbines

CHAPTER 3

HOW DOES HYDROPOWER COMPARE?

Power plants powered by fossil fuels release harmful chemicals into the air.

People have burned fossil fuels to make energy for many years. These fuels provide power for electricity and transportation, but they have drawbacks. Burning coal, oil, and natural gas pollutes the air and makes people sick. Coal dust can cause illness in people who work in mines or live nearby. Leaks from oil pipelines or tanker ships can damage the environment and kill wildlife. Natural gas catches on fire easily, which makes it dangerous to **transport**. Plus, fossil fuels will someday run out. Renewable energy sources are available, safe, and better for the environment. They are also becoming more affordable.

transport—to move or carry something or someone from one place to another

Killer Oil Spill

The world's largest oil spill happened in 1991 in the Persian Gulf. One barrel of crude oil holds 42 gallons (159 liters). About 10 million barrels of oil spilled across 100 miles (161 kilometers) long and 40 miles (64 km) wide. The oil killed countless fish and about 30,000 water birds.

Hydropower now supplies 71 percent of the world's renewable electricity. It has been used for many years, so people trust it. It is also one of the cheapest ways to produce power. Yet, like any power source, it has both advantages and disadvantages.

POSITIVES OF HYDROPOWER

Hydropower has many benefits. It's fueled by water, so it doesn't pollute the air like power plants that burn fossil fuels do. Hydropower is also flexible. Water flow can be adjusted to create a little power or a lot of it. An area with a hydropower plant can produce its own energy. That means residents do not have to rely on fuel being transported from other states or countries. This cuts down on pollution as well.

The Riga Electric Hydropower Plant in Latvia has been in operation since the 1970s.

NEGATIVES OF HYDROPOWER

Hydropower isn't a perfect energy source. It takes lots of water and land to build a hydropower plant. To build reservoirs, land must be flooded. If people live on that land, they must move from their homes. Once a good location has been found, the cost to build the plant can be quite expensive. It can reach billions of dollars.

Hydropower is also dependent on the weather cycle. Power can't be produced when there's a long dry spell.

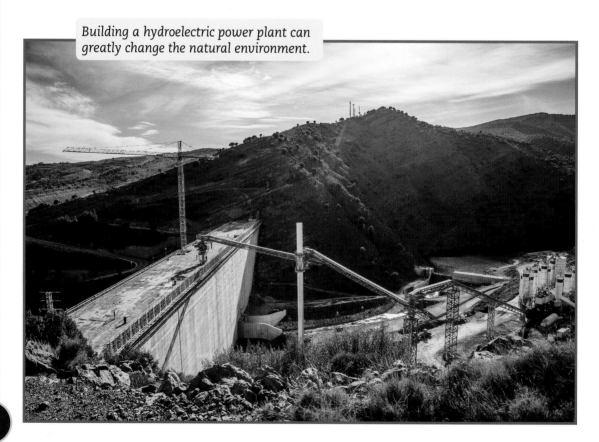

Building a hydroelectric power plant can greatly change the natural environment.

Fish such as salmon swim upstream to lay their eggs.

Many people also have concerns about the ways hydropower plants affect the environment. Dams can raise river temperatures. The warmer water may kill off certain types of plants and fish. Dams also interfere with some fish **migration**. When these fish can't swim up or down stream, they can't **reproduce**.

. . . .

migration—the regular movement of animals from one place to another

reproduce—to breed and have offspring

HELPING FISH AROUND DAMS

If fish can't swim to where they need to go, they may get sick or not be able to reproduce. Entire species can die off. But scientists are working to solve this problem.

Fish ladders provide **detours** around dams. The ladders contain a series of small pools laid out like stairs. Fish leap through gushing water and land in a pool. They rest there for a while before leaping into the next pool. They repeat the process until they are past the dam.

Fish elevators can also help fish get around dams. Fish swim into a container at the base of a dam. When enough fish gather, the container carries them over the dam. The fish are then released.

Fish ladders are part of the Bonneville Dam in Oregon.

detour—a path to travel on when the usual way of traveling cannot be used

The fish ladder at this hydroelectric power plant in Germany creates a path that makes it easier for the fish to follow.

Many Uses for Dams

In the United States, only 2,400 of the country's 80,000 dams make electricity. So what are all those other dams used for? Many dams hold local water supplies. This water may be cleaned and used for drinking and bathing. They can provide water for swimming, boating, or for farmers to water their crops. Some dams raise water levels enough so that ships can travel where it would otherwise be too shallow. Other dams work to prevent floods. During heavy rains, dam gates can be closed to store water in the reservoir. During dry weather, gates can be opened to release water and raise river levels.

CHAPTER 4

HOW AND WHERE IS HYDROPOWER USED?

Hydropower is the most widely used renewable energy source. About 70 percent of the world's renewable energy comes from hydropower. More than 150 countries create it. China makes more hydroelectricity than any other country. Hydropower makes one-fifth of all electricity in the world.

Top Hydropower-Generating Countries

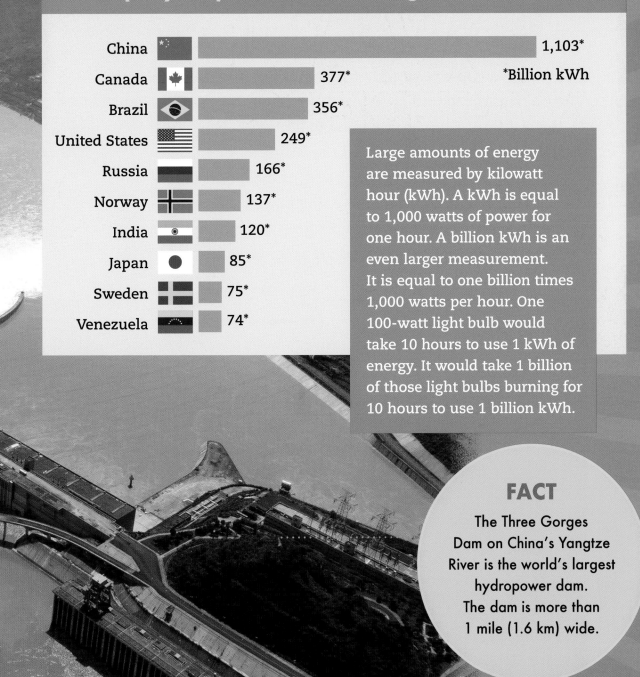

Country	Billion kWh
China	1,103*
Canada	377*
Brazil	356*
United States	249*
Russia	166*
Norway	137*
India	120*
Japan	85*
Sweden	75*
Venezuela	74*

*Billion kWh

Large amounts of energy are measured by kilowatt hour (kWh). A kWh is equal to 1,000 watts of power for one hour. A billion kWh is an even larger measurement. It is equal to one billion times 1,000 watts per hour. One 100-watt light bulb would take 10 hours to use 1 kWh of energy. It would take 1 billion of those light bulbs burning for 10 hours to use 1 billion kWh.

FACT

The Three Gorges Dam on China's Yangtze River is the world's largest hydropower dam. The dam is more than 1 mile (1.6 km) wide.

LOOKING TO THE FUTURE

Many people want to reduce pollution and protect natural resources. They turn to renewable energy sources to help in these efforts. Hydropower soon will play an even larger role in making energy throughout the world.

Hydroelectric dams sit on some of the world's most powerful rivers. Yet there are many places where new dams can be built. Central America, South America, central Africa, India, and China may be good areas for growth.

Many more hydroelectric dams like this one in Ecuador are being planned along the Amazon River in South America.

The U.S. Department of Energy also expects growth. In 2017 about 7 percent of U.S. electricity came from hydropower. The United States government wants that amount to double by 2030.

Scientists and engineers are experimenting with better ways to build dams and make more power with existing dams. New turbines are being designed to safely make more power. Researchers are trying to add turbines to dams that weren't built for power. Others are working on ways to use ocean waves to make electricity. As technology improves, hydropower will be even more available and affordable.

In Norway, wave converters are already providing electricity for citizens.

COULD YOU WORK AT A HYDROPOWER PLANT?

In 2016 more than 8 million people worldwide worked in the renewable energy field. This number is expected to keep growing. Could you be one of those people someday?

Many engineers and electricians are needed to work at hydropower plants. Workers are needed to keep the plant running smoothly and repair equipment. Many of these jobs require college degrees in fields such as engineering or physics. Taking math and science classes now can help you decide if you like these subjects.

Hydropower plants also hire support staff. These employees don't run the turbines, but their work is important. For example, wildlife biologists make sure the plants do not harm fish or animals. Recreation employees design programs for boaters and swimmers to enjoy the water without interfering with dam operation. There are also spokespeople to share messages about the plant. If you want to work at a hydropower plant one day, there are many possibilities!

FACT

The hydrolectricity industry is growing fast. Projections show it could double by the year 2050.

GLOSSARY

detour (DEE-toor)—a path to travel on when the usual way of traveling cannot be used

generator (JEN-uh-ray-tur)—a machine used to convert mechanical energy into electricity

migration (mye-GRAY-shuhn)—the regular movement of animals from one place to another

renewable (ri-NOO-uh-buhl)—describes power from sources that you can use over and over again that cannot be used up, such as wind, water, and the sun

reproduce (ree-pruh-DOOSE)—to breed and have offspring

transformer (transs-FOR-mur)—a device that changes the voltage of an electrical current

transport (transs-PORT)—to move or carry something or someone from one place to another

turbine (TUR-bine)—a machine with blades that can be turned by a moving fluid such as steam or water

vapor (VAY-pur)—a gas made from a liquid

READ MORE

Bailey, Diane. *Hydropower.* Harnessing Energy. Mankato, Minn.: Creative Education, 2015.

Dickmann, Nancy. *Energy From Water: Hydroelectric, Tidal, and Wave Power.* Next Generation Energy. St. Catharines, Ontario; New York: Crabtree Publishing Company, 2016.

Labrecque, Ellen. *Renewable Energy.* Global Citizens. Environmentalism. North Ann Arbor, Mich.: Cherry Lake Publishing, 2018.

INTERNET SITES

Use FactHound to find Internet sites related to this book.

Visit www.facthound.com

Just type in 9781543555431 and go.

Check out projects, games and lots more at
www.capstonekids.com

CRITICAL THINKING QUESTIONS

1. More than 75 percent of the world's energy still comes from fossil fuels. Why don't more countries rely upon renewable energy sources such as hydropower?

2. What do you think will happen if people keep using fossil fuels instead of renewable energy sources?

3. There are pros and cons to using hydropower. Do you think the advantages outweigh the disadvantages?

INDEX